Cyrus

Araxes

CASPIAN SEA

Lake
Van

Lake
Urmia

MEDIA

ELBURZ MOUNTAINS

ASSYRIA • Nineveh

Ashur •

Tigris

MESOPOTAMIA

ZAGROS MOUNTAINS

The hanging gardens of
Babylon

Babylon •

Kish •

Susa •

BABYLONIA

ELAM

DESERT

Erech •
Ur •

The Ziggurat at Ur (a
famous temple-tower)

ARABIAN GULF

Living Stories from the Bible

MOSES
Leader of a Nation

Hutchinson
London Melbourne Sydney Auckland Johannesburg

Foreword

THERE IS A SENSE IN WHICH THE BIBLE has to be rewritten for every generation. Otherwise it becomes a relic of the past, an ancient book encased in black covers and exclusively associated with the Church. But the Bible is for all mankind, young and old, black and white, 20th century or 1st century. This new publication fulfils the purpose which animated those who produced it, i.e. to make the Bible live for the young (and the young in heart) in the way in which it has lived in the hearts and minds of men for 2000 years and more. The stories are vividly (and accurately) told; the illustrations are magnificent and the literary format easy to follow. I congratulate the authors, the illustrators and the publishers on a singularly attractive publication.

Stuart Ebor: (Archbishop of York)

THE BIBLE HAS TO BE SEEN, not so much as history to be studied, as an invitation to God's way of life for us. Various literary forms are used and it is important that from an early age we are enabled to understand their meaning. In presentation to children, the Old Testament books are perhaps inevitably taken more or less literally. But here a fair balance has been preserved and the adaptation of the New Testament material shows considerable skill and sensitivity. With the exciting illustrations, the whole should do much to develop among young readers an interest in the Bible which should lead to a developing love and appreciation for the history of man's salvation.

†Derek Worlock (Roman Catholic
Archbishop of Liverpool)

AUTHORS
Meryl and Malcolm Doney

EDITOR
John Grisewood

DESIGNER
John Strange

ARTISTS
Harry Bishop **Doug Post**
Martin Reiner **Tudor Art**

OLD TESTAMENT CONSULTANT
Alan Millard
Rankin Senior Lecturer in Hebrew and Ancient Semitic Languages University of Liverpool

ADVISORY PANEL
Reverend John Huxtable DD
Reverend Gilbert Kirby
Sister Mary Richardson

Published by Hutchinson Junior Books Ltd
3 Fitzroy Square London W1
An imprint of the Hutchinson Publishing Group

First published 1980

Designed and produced by Grisewood & Dempsey Ltd
Grosvenor House, 141/143 Drury Lane, London WC2

ISBN 0 09 141710 4

© Grisewood & Dempsey Ltd 1980

Printed and bound by Tien Wah Press (Pte) Singapore

Contents

The Bible extracts used in this series are from the Revised Standard Version, copy-righted 1946, 1952, © 1971, 1973.

The Family that became a Nation

MUCH OF THE OLD TESTAMENT is a history of the Hebrews, or Israelites. But it is not mere history, not just a chronicle of important events. It is history written with a special purpose: a record of God's activity in the world and the working of his will in the lives of men and women so that mankind shall be saved.

The story in this book tells of a family that became a great nation. It is told in the first two books of the Old Testament, Genesis and Exodus.

The story begins in a damp dungeon in Ancient Egypt, where a young man is held captive. His name is Joseph and he is one of Jacob's sons.

Jacob's family has a remarkable history. Years earlier, Jacob's grandfather, Abraham, was told by God to leave the thriving city of Ur in Mesopotamia and set out for Canaan (modern Israel). God told him that he would found a new nation based on his family.

By the time of Jacob and his sons, the family had grown and settled in the land God had given them. There God began to mould them into his own special people. Then a terrible famine threatened to destroy them. But God had already made plans to save them. Joseph, shut away in prison in Egypt, was part of that plan.

In these stories you will follow Joseph's dealings with his once treacherous brothers and see the Hebrews grow into a strong tribe, far from their homeland. But their fortunes change and they are forced into slavery. God rescues them again by sending a powerful leader – Moses.

You will read how Moses defies the Pharaoh and leads the Israelites into the desert; and learn how God cares for his people during their wanderings, saving them from enemies, and then from hunger and thirst. The Israelites slowly learn who their God is and how he wants them to live. The once small tribe has become a great nation, ready to enter the Promised Land where new adventures await them. But that is another story.

Pharaoh's Dream

PHARAOH, THE KING OF EGYPT, was not sleeping at all well. He was having a nightmare. He dreamt he saw seven fat, healthy cows climb out of the river Nile and stand peacefully cropping the grass on the bank. Then a strange thing happened. Seven more cows climbed out of the water. But they were thin and looked like skeletons. Instead of eating the grass, they swallowed the seven fat cows; but still they looked thin.

Pharaoh woke up in a cold sweat. What did this strange disturbing dream mean? Puzzled, he tried to go back to sleep. But he had a second dream. This time he saw seven fat ears of corn growing on a stalk in a field. Then another stalk sprouted out of the ground with seven, thin dry ears of corn on it. As before with the cows, the thin corn swallowed the fat corn. Pharaoh woke up. He was frightened. He was sure his dreams had a meaning, but he could not think what it was.

In the morning he called his cleverest advisers and magicians. He told them about his dreams and demanded to know what they meant. But his advisers had to admit that they did not know. Pharaoh sent them away in disgust.

Then Pharaoh's butler came to him, half-afraid to speak. "Sir," he said, "do you remember when you were displeased with me and put me in prison? There was another prisoner there and we both had strange dreams. A young Hebrew, also a prisoner, told us their meaning. Both our dreams came true; just as he foretold. I was reinstated in your service and the other man was hanged." When Pharaoh heard this, he decided he would send for the young Hebrew. His name was Joseph.

Joseph had been born and brought up in Canaan, a country to the north east of Egypt. He was the son of Jacob, a descendant of Abraham and therefore one of God's chosen people, the Hebrews. God's special name for Jacob was Israel. So, his family became known as Israelites.

Jacob had twelve sons, but Joseph was his favourite. Because of this, Joseph's ten elder brothers hated him. And when Joseph began to have strange dreams in which the whole world, including his parents and brothers, were bowing down before him, they hated him even more. They would like to have killed him, but instead decided to sell him as a slave. They told their father that Joseph had been killed by a wild animal while looking after the family sheep.

So Joseph was sold into slavery in Egypt. But God was with him and he became a successful man, then his master's wife plotted against him and Joseph was put into prison.

The order was sent to the prison; Pharaoh wanted to see Joseph. Joseph changed his clothes and was ushered into the presence of the King.

Joseph prayed silently to God as he listened to Pharaoh's account of his dreams. He knew immediately what they meant. "Your dreams have the same meaning," he said. "The seven fat cows and the seven ears of corn represent seven years of good weather and bumper harvests. The seven thin cows and the seven poor ears of corn represent seven years of terrible famine that will follow. The thin cows did not become fatter in your dream because the famine will be so great that it will wipe out even the memory of all the years of plenty. God was speaking to you through those nightmares."

Pharaoh was pleased to have his dreams interpreted, but he was horrified at their meaning. Joseph then told the Pharaoh of a plan to save the country and its people. "Choose a sensible and intelligent man and put him in charge of the country and its farming," he said. "Throughout the seven years of plenty he and his managers will collect one fifth of all the food grown and store it in the cities. Then there will be enough for everyone during the shortage of the next seven years."

Pharaoh was so impressed by Joseph's interpretation and his splendid plan, that he put him in charge of carrying it out immediately. His power was second only to the Pharaoh himself.

So Joseph took a fifth of all the country's produce during the seven years of good harvests and stored it away in silos. He soon had trained overseers to make sure that the work was done well. Joseph was only 30 years old; a very young age for such an important position. But he firmly believed God had given him the work to do and would help him.

Genesis 41

Joseph's Brothers

JUST AS JOSEPH HAD FORETOLD, a more unsettled period began after the seven years of good harvests. There were storms and drought, crops grew badly and harvests were poor.

Soon the Egyptians began to run out of food. "Help us, Pharaoh, we're getting hungry," they cried. "You go and ask Joseph what to do," Pharaoh told them. When the food shortage had become really severe Joseph opened up the great storehouses and sold supplies to all who needed them. His plan was a great success.

Not only Egypt, but all the surrounding countries were also suffering from famine. Before long people came from everywhere to buy grain, including Canaan where Joseph's own family were badly short of food. Joseph's father, Jacob, told ten of his sons to go to Egypt to buy grain.

Joseph's brothers looked nervously at one another. When they had sold their brother, the traders had taken him to Egypt. What if he was still there? Jacob didn't understand why they looked guilty. He sent them off on the long journey – all except his youngest son Benjamin.

When the brothers arrived in Egypt they were told to go to Joseph, who directed all selling of grain to foreigners. But they did not recognize their young brother. He was clean shaven like an Egyptian and wore fine clothes and rare jewels. They bowed down before him in respect.

Joseph knew who they were immediately. In the shock of seeing them he decided not to tell them who he was. He would test them to see if they felt sorry for what they had done to him. He treated them like strangers and spoke harshly to them. Pretending he did not understand their language, he spoke to them through an interpreter. "You are spies. You have come to see how weak we are."

The brothers were horrified. This man had the power to kill them as spies. "No, no" they protested. "We are not spies. We have come to buy grain. We are ten of twelve brothers. One brother is at home, the other one is dead". Joseph pretended he did not believe them. They were put in prison and questioned for three days about the family history, including what they had done to their brother Joseph.

On the third day he released them. "I am a God-fearing man," he said. "I will give you the chance to prove that you are honest. One of you will stay here in prison while the others return home with the grain. But you must bring back with you the youngest brother you have told me about".

The brothers were frightened and felt guilty. "We're in trouble with this man because of what we did to Joseph," they said. "It's God's way of punishing us". Joseph sat listening to them. Now he knew that they were sorry for what they had done to him.

But Joseph had not finished with them yet. He kept his brother, Simeon, in gaol, and before the brothers set out for home he secretly put the money they had given him for the grain back into the sacks on their pack donkeys.

On the way home the brothers stopped for the night and one of them opened a sack to feed his donkey. There, on top of the grain, was the money bag. How had it got there? Perhaps the Egyptian was trying to trick them so that he would have an excuse to kill them all.

The frightened group of brothers arrived home and told their father Jacob everything that had happened. When they emptied the rest of the grain sacks to show him what they had bought, out fell the other money bags! Jacob was angry and shouted at them, "Last time you went away you came back without Joseph and now you come back without Simeon. Then you tell me you want to take Benjamin, my youngest son." Jacob refused to send Benjamin back to Egypt with his brothers. He still mourned for Joseph and he was not going to let his new favourite leave his side. *Genesis 42*

The Silver Cup

JACOB HOPED THAT THE FAMINE would soon stop, and that rain and good crops would come again. But they did not. Before long all the grain the brothers had brought from Egypt was gone. So their father told them: "You will have to go to Egypt again to buy us more food."

Judah reminded him of their last visit. "You realize we will have to take Benjamin with us. The Egyptian was serious when he said, 'Don't come back without your brother.'" Jacob remembered the terms. "Why did you tell him about Ben-jamin?" he asked bitterly. "We had no idea he would want to see him," they replied. Judah tried to reassure his father, promising to take special care of the favourite son.

Reluctantly Jacob agreed. "Take as many gifts as we can afford," he said. "Honey, spices, balm, pistachio nuts and almonds, the best the land can provide. Take twice as much money this time, so that you can pay back what was left in your sacks". And, although it was hard for the old man, he said: "Take Benjamin with you too. I pray that God will allow you to bring him and Simeon back alive."

So the brothers set off with their laden pack-donkeys. They were again presented to Joseph. He invited them to eat with him at his private house at noon. While he had gone to instruct his stewards to prepare a feast, the brothers looked at one another

nervously. "Why should he want us to come to his private house? He must think we stole the money we found and is going to make us slaves."

At Joseph's palace they went straight to his household manager and told him their worries. "On our way back home last time," they said, "we found our money still in our sacks. We don't know how it got there. We didn't steal it. We've brought it back as well as more money to pay for more grain." Joseph's manager looked at them kindly. "Don't worry," he said, "That money must have been a gift from God, because our books say that the grain was paid for!"

Joseph arrived at his palace at noon and the brothers gave him their presents. Joseph was pleased. He asked as casually as he could, after his father, and was specially kind to Benjamin. He gave

him five times more food than anyone else. Simeon was released from prison and joined them. The brothers began to enjoy the feast.

But Joseph had not finished with his brothers – not yet. When they were ready to leave, he told his steward to fill their sacks with all the grain they could carry and once again to put back the money that had been paid. And this time, on the orders of his master, the manager put Joseph's own silver cup in the top of Benjamin's sack.

After they had left, Joseph flew into a mock rage, accusing them of taking advantage of his kindness by stealing from him. He ordered his men to saddle up their horses and pursue the brothers. Joseph's men overtook the caravan and brought it to a halt.

"Who do you take us for?" the brothers demanded. "We've already tried to return the money we found. Do you think we would then go back and steal from your master again?" But they had to allow their sacks to be searched, from the oldest brother down to the youngest. Of course Joseph's men found the money in the top of each sack, and last of all, when Benjamin's sack was opened, out fell Joseph's silver cup! Once more the brothers were shocked and afraid. What were they to do? They might as well be dead. In despair they reloaded the sacks and headed back to the city and slavery.

Joseph was waiting for them. He pretended to be angry. "What can we say to prove we are innocent?" they pleaded. "This must be God's punishment for our evil past. Take us as your slaves." But Joseph said, "I'll only take the one who stole my cup." Desperately, Judah spoke up "Please, don't take Benjamin. If you made him a slave his father would die of sorrow. Let me stay as your slave instead."

Joseph ordered his attendants out of the room so that he could be alone with his brothers. Then he broke down in tears. "I am your brother Joseph!" he said. His brothers were amazed.

"Don't feel guilty about what you did to me," Joseph went on: "It was part of God's plan. He has given me this position so that I can look after our people in these hard times. He wants us all to stay alive because we are the beginning of a great nation – his people. I want you to go back home and fetch our father and come and live here with me." Then he hugged and kissed them all. When the brothers finally found their voices, they poured out their relief and joy. *Genesis 43–45*

13

Joseph's family moves to Egypt

BEFORE LONG EVERYONE in Joseph's household knew that he had been reunited with his family. The Egyptians were overjoyed for him. When Pharaoh heard, he was pleased too. He insisted that Joseph send for his father and promised he would be given the best land and all the privileges of an honoured citizen.

Joseph's brothers set off for Canaan as soon as they could. When they arrived they broke the news to their father Jacob. "Joseph did not die. He is alive and in charge of the whole of Egypt!" Jacob did not know what to think. He was no longer sure he could trust his sons. But when they told him everything that had happened, and he saw the wagonloads of food that Joseph had sent with them, he realized that they must be telling the truth. Then it dawned on him that he was going to see his long-lost son again. "My son is alive," he shouted. Immediately he began to prepare for the journey to Egypt. Jacob was now an old man and he must see his son again before he died.

They set off on the long, slow journey. This time the whole tribe went – wives, children, servants, together with their flocks of sheep and cattle.

On the way the great caravan stopped at Beer-sheba, on the borders of Canaan, to offer sacrifices to God. That night God spoke to Jacob in a dream. "Do not be afraid to go to Egypt, for I promise that your family will be the beginning of a great nation and I will bring your descendants back to their homeland. You, Jacob, will die in Egypt with Joseph at your side."

In time they arrived in Egypt. They made their way to see Joseph. When he saw his father, Joseph was overcome by emotion. They fell into one another's arms and wept with joy. Later, Joseph introduced his father and some of his brothers to Pharaoh, who treated them well and gave them much valuable land on which to live and rear their livestock.

While Joseph's family settled into their new home, Joseph was kept busy with affairs of state. The famine was still raging and the people of Egypt were rapidly using up the grain from the city storehouses. Until now, people had paid for the grain, but before long most families had no money left. They pleaded: "You must let us have grain or we shall die!" So Joseph decided to take livestock in exchange for the grain. The seven years of famine dragged on and eventually there were no sheep, oxen or donkeys left to exchange. So Joseph accepted land in payment, until all the cultivated land in Egypt belonged to the Pharaoh.

However, Joseph soon realized that this policy would not be good for Egypt. When better times came, the people would have no land to cultivate to support themselves. So Joseph devised a new plan. He leased the land back to the people, announcing, "You may cultivate the leased land and I will give you seed to sow. When it is harvested, you may keep four-fifths of the crops to live on and to sow again. The other fifth must be paid to Pharaoh."

Joseph's decision changed the whole way of life in Egypt for a long time. It led to a strong and wealthy ruling family but also saved the lives of the Egyptian farmers and the many foreigners who came to Egypt to buy grain.

Jacob lived for another 17 years. He saw his family become well established and prosperous in the new country. It grew into a huge tribe. When Jacob died at a great age, the whole nation went into mourning for 70 days. Jacob's body was taken to Canaan to be buried as he had requested.

When Joseph's brothers returned from burying their father, some of their old fears revived. What if Joseph still harboured a grudge? But Joseph reassured them. He had forgiven them completely.

Later Joseph took them into his confidence. "Soon I am going to die," he said, "but God has promised that in his own time he will take our family out of Egypt, back to the Promised Land."

When Joseph died, his body was embalmed in the Egyptian way and kept as a treasured possession. One day they would take it with them and bury Joseph in Canaan, the Promised Land.
Genesis 46–50

The Early Life of Moses

JACOB'S FAMILY LIVED VERY WELL in Egypt. After Joseph's death, Pharaoh allowed them to stay on as a separate tribe, giving them the land called Goshen in which to live. They grew in numbers, and adapted well to the settled life of Egypt.

Three hundred peaceful years passed. Then a Pharaoh came to the throne who thought it was dangerous to have such a large and prosperous immigrant community living among his own people. At any time they could ally themselves to a foreign power and overthrow the government.

Pharaoh had large building projects in mind, and here was a ready-made labour force. So instead of allowing the Israelites the freedom to work their own land as before, he passed new laws making them slaves to the Egyptians.

Building in Egypt was done entirely by hand, using thousands of workers. It was tough work for even the fittest. The work-gangs were driven by

task-masters who flogged anyone who slackened. Life had become unbearable for the Israelites.

Pharaoh then decided on more drastic action. As the tribe continued to grow alarmingly, he appointed two Egyptian women to help as midwives to the Hebrews. He ordered them to kill every baby boy they delivered. Bravely, the women refused. They feared God and they would do nothing to harm his chosen people.

Angrily, Pharaoh issued orders to his people. All baby boys born to Israelites must be thrown into the Nile and drowned. The Israelites were angry and horrified at this new order. Parents tried to hide their babies from the authorities, but many were drowned. One couple, descendants of Joseph's brother, Levi, managed to save their son. They hid the baby boy for three months and then made a waterproof basket for him out of reeds and pitch. They put the baby into it and then gently floated it among the tall reeds at the edge of the river, hoping some kind Egyptian might find him, take pity and care for him.

But the baby was not alone. His sister hid in the reeds to see what happened. As she watched, one of Pharaoh's daughters came down to the river to bathe. Suddenly, she noticed the basket and sent one of her maids to get it. As they opened the basket the baby began to cry. Her heart warmed to the little boy and she realized that he must be one of the Israelite babies.

His sister rushed up to the Pharaoh's daughter. "Would you like someone to look after him for you until he is weaned?" she asked. "I know someone who would." Pharaoh's daughter agreed and the little girl ran to fetch her mother. Not knowing that she was the baby's real mother, Pharaoh's daughter offered her wages to look after him. So the family was able to care for him until he was a small boy.

Then, sadly, his mother had to take him to Pharaoh's court where he would be brought up as if he were part of the royal family. There, Pharaoh's daughter gave him the name Moses, which means "drawn from the water".

Moses lived the life of a king's son in the Egyptian court until he was about 40. But as time passed he became more and more interested in his own people. One day, while he was out watching his countrymen at their work, he saw one of the Egyptian task-masters beating up a poor Israelite slave. Moses was angry. He looked about him carefully to make sure nobody was watching. Then he attacked the Egyptian and killed him, hastily burying his body in the sand.

The next day Moses saw one of the slaves pick a fight with another. Moses intervened. He was unhappy that two of his countrymen should quarrel. Turning to the man who started it he said, "Why are you fighting with a fellow Hebrew?" "Who do you think you are," he returned, "that you should tell us what to do? Are you going to kill us as you killed the Egyptian yesterday?" Moses' heart missed a beat. Everyone must know what he had done.

The word soon got back to Pharaoh. He was very angry that the Israelite who had been brought up in his court should turn against him. He ordered his men to find and kill Moses.

Moses was now on the run for his life. He gathered a few belongings together and fled away from Egypt. He came to a desert land where the only people were Midianites, a semi-nomadic tribe also descended from Abraham. He was taken in by the family of a man named Jethro and worked for him as a shepherd. Eventually, Moses married one of his daughters, Zipporah, and settled into the new desert life.

In time Pharaoh died, but the Israelites were still slaves. They cried out to God to help them. As he had promised to Joseph, years before, God was preparing a leader for his people, who would take them back to their own land. That leader was to be Moses. *Exodus 1–2*

The Burning Bush

WHILE MOSES WAS ON THE SLOPES of Mount Sinai one day looking after his father-in-law's sheep, he saw a strange sight. At first glance it looked like an ordinary bush fire. In the dry desert region it was a common thing for a single bush to burst into flames. But there was something strange about this fire. The branches appeared to be burning but the flames did not destroy them. Moses went up for a closer look and heard a voice speaking from the fire! Moses was astounded. It was the voice of God. "Moses, Moses," he heard. Moses replied "Yes, here I am." "Take off your shoes, this is holy ground", came the voice again. Moses did so, turning his face away from the blaze, afraid to look.

The voice said: "I am the God of your ancestors, Abraham, Isaac and Jacob. I know what your countrymen are suffering in Egypt and I have heard their cries for help. I am going to bring them out into a land of their own. I want you to lead them."

Moses remembered that he had not been accepted by the slaves. He said, "They will not listen to me. They will want to know who sent me." God said "Tell them my name. My name is I AM. Say I AM has sent me to you and that I promise to take them to Canaan. They will listen to you. Take the elders with you when you appear before Pharaoh and demand to be allowed to go out into the desert to make sacrifices to me. The king will not allow it unless he is forced to, but I will show my power against him and in the end he will let you go."

Moses still had objections. "They will never believe you told me this." So God gave him the power to do three miracles that would convince the people of his authority. First he told Moses to throw his walking staff to the ground. As he did so it became a poisonous snake, writhing in the sand! Moses picked it up gingerly and to his relief it became a staff again.

God then commanded Moses to put his hand into his robe next to his skin. When he brought it out, it was horribly diseased with leprosy! "Put your hand back into your robe," God commanded and when Moses brought it out again, it was healed. God continued: "If the Israelites do not believe you after these two miracles, pour some water from the river Nile on the ground and it will turn into blood."

Moses was convinced by these signs but he still felt unable to face Pharaoh. "Lord", he said, "I cannot make great speeches. I am slow and hesitant and am often at a loss for words." God said, "Who makes people's mouths? I do! I will help you speak and tell you what to say."

By now Moses was afraid. "Please!" he pleaded, "send someone else." God became angry at Moses' stubbornness and disobedience. "Your brother Aaron is a good speaker. At this moment he is on his way here to find you. I will help both of you to speak well for me. He will be your spokesman, but you will be my mouthpiece to tell him what to say. Now go, and take your staff with you, so that you can do the signs I showed you."

As the fire in the bush died away, Moses turned to go. God had chosen his leader and although Moses was still afraid, he was also excited. A great adventure had begun. *Exodus 3–4*

"Let my People Go"

WITH GOD'S SPECIAL COMMISSION still echoing in his mind, Moses went back to his father-in-law and asked if he could return to Egypt. Jethro gave his blessing and Moses set off with his wife and sons. As God had foretold, Moses met his brother Aaron in the desert and explained to him everything that God had told him.

When they arrived in Egypt, they called a meeting of all the elders of the Hebrew families. Aaron acted as Moses' spokesman and Moses performed the miracles God had shown him. Seeing Moses' power and hearing God's promise to rescue them, the elders were overjoyed and happily accepted the brothers as their leaders.

When the time came, it took a year of disasters to accomplish God's plan, a year in which Moses and Aaron were continually put to the test.

To begin with, Moses and Aaron, full of confidence in God's power, appeared before Pharaoh and told him God's message. "The God of Israel says 'Let my people go, so that they can hold a festival in the desert to honour me.'" Pharaoh refused.

"Who is this God that I should take any notice of him? I will not let the people go," he shouted. "Your people are obviously not working hard enough if you have time for festivals."

Pharaoh decided to make things even harder for the Hebrews. One of the slaves' jobs was to make bricks for building. Normally they were given straw to mix with the clay before the bricks were baked. Pharaoh now ordered the slaves to find their own straw, but to make exactly the same number of bricks each day.

In desperation a deputation of foremen came to Pharaoh and pleaded with him to be reasonable. "If you have time to go and worship your God," Pharaoh replied, "you're obviously not working hard enough. Get on with it."

The miserable foremen turned on Moses and Aaron. "We hope God punishes you for what you've done!" they said bitterly." Because of you, Pharaoh hates us and now has an excuse to kill us."

Moses was shocked. Silently he prayed to God. "How can you do this to your people? In sending me to Pharaoh you have made things even harder than before."

But God was patient with Moses. "Wait and see what I will do," he said. "In the end Pharaoh will drive you out of the land."

So Moses went back to the elders and tried to encourage them by telling them what God was going to do. But they were so dispirited they found it hard to believe Moses.

Summoning all their courage and faith Moses and Aaron asked for a second audience with the Pharaoh. Once more they told the King that they wanted to take all their belongings and travel three days into the desert to worship God. To prove their authority to be God's spokesmen, Aaron threw his staff down, as God had shown Moses. Immediately, it became a snake. But Egyptian courts were used to such signs. Pharaoh called his sorcerers, who by the skilled use of magic, were able to do similar things. Their staffs, too, appeared to become snakes and for one terrible moment the palace floor was crawling with them. As everyone watched open mouthed, Aaron's snake swallowed up all the others. Pharaoh looked at the brothers with new respect but he would not change his mind.

God now told Moses to meet the king by the river Nile the next morning. As Pharaoh and his court appeared, Aaron stepped up to him and said "Now God will show you who he is by what he does to your land." He raised the staff in his hand and brought it down hard on the surface of the river. Slowly, the Nile turned blood red. Soon the water was so polluted that all the fish died. The court sorcerers, anxious about their jobs, convinced Pharaoh that they could do the same thing by magic. So Pharaoh remained stubborn. But for seven days the water of the Nile was undrinkable.

This disaster was just the first of a series. Driven from the water by the rotting fish, millions of frogs left the rivers and canals and hopped about the land. People found them everywhere. Once again, Pharaoh's magicians made light of the problem, but Pharaoh was beginning to feel uneasy. This God was a powerful enemy. "All right," he said to Moses, "Ask your God to take the frogs away and I'll let you go."

Moses prayed and God did as Moses asked. The frogs on the land died. But Pharaoh again refused to listen to Moses and Aaron.

God told Moses that Aaron should strike the ground with his staff. As Aaron did so swarms of mosquitoes spread over the land, covering animals and people like dust. The people itched, and scratched themselves. This time the magicians were beaten; they could not make mosquitoes appear by magic. But Pharaoh was still stubborn.

To add to the misery caused by the mosquitoes swarms of flies now infested Egypt, except for Goshen where the Israelites lived. Pharaoh tried to persuade Moses to agree to make his sacrifices in Egypt, but Moses refused. "Our sacrifices of animals offend your people," he said. "We would be in danger of being stoned by them. We must go into the desert." Pharaoh finally relented. He said that the Israelites could go into the desert, but not very far, if Moses made the wretched flies go away. Moses prayed to God and the flies went. But Pharaoh broke his word again.

By now Egypt was in a very bad way. God promised, through Moses and Aaron, that there would be more plagues. An epidemic spread like wildfire through the Egyptian cattle and many of them became sick and died. The Israelite livestock remained perfectly healthy, showing that God was protecting Israel. Yet still Pharaoh was stubborn and refused to let the people go.

Finally, infection spread to the people. Moses and Aaron, on God's instructions, showed Pharaoh what was to happen by taking handfuls of ash and throwing it up in the air. The ashes floated down

Plagues

The terrible plagues which afflicted the Egyptians for a year and which in the end persuaded Pharaoh to set free the Hebrew slaves may well have had quite natural causes: the Nile in flood does look reddish from the sediment that is swept in its course; the blotting out of sunlight may have been caused by a sandstorm; locusts still often swarm in the area; and the death of the first-born may have been an epidemic. But what the author of the story wishes to show is that God's actions are accomplished through nature. In the same way God chose as his mouthpiece, a man – Moses. Moses must have been a great leader because he always appears as the central character in the popular stories which the Hebrews handed down from generation to generation about their escape from slavery and of their march into their homeland.

like a fine dust. As the dust settled, people and animals became badly infected with boils. Pharaoh still refused to listen.

The next warning God gave, included a way out for those Egyptians who believed he would carry out his threats. Through the two brothers, he warned of a great hail storm, with stones so big they could kill. Some of the Egyptians were sensible and took the warning seriously. They shut up their animals and rushed indoors. Others took no notice and went about their business as usual.

The storm was indeed the worst Egypt had ever known. The flax and barley crops, nearly ready for harvesting, were flattened by hailstones. The one place the storm missed was Goshen.

Pharaoh was beginning to get the point. He told Moses: "I have done wrong, so have my people. Your God is in the right. Ask him to stop this awful storm and your people can go."

Moses knew that Pharaoh did not yet truly fear God. But he did as Pharaoh asked. As he prayed, the storm stopped. Pharaoh breathed a sigh of relief and tried to negotiate with the Israelites. "Just who is going on this holiday?" he asked. "All of us," replied Moses. "I knew it!" burst out Pharaoh. "You are planning to revolt, not worship. You are going to leave Egypt. I will not allow it". "Then see what the Lord will do," replied Moses.

The Egyptian wheat crop had survived the storms because it was not ripe. Just as it became ready for harvest a great cloud of locusts, carried on an east wind, hit Egypt. The wheat fields were blackened by them. They ate everything the hail had left. Egypt's economy was in ruins. Pharaoh pleaded for the locusts to be removed. When they were, he sent Moses and Aaron away again.

So God plunged the whole land into darkness. A thick dust storm blanketed out the sun's light. The Egyptians could see nothing for three whole days, and they were very frightened. They worshipped Ra, the Sun god, and took this as a sign that he had been destroyed. In the darkness Pharaoh tried one last ploy.

The Israelites could all go into the desert, but they were to leave their cattle behind. Moses refused. It was their privilege, he said, to choose their own animals for sacrifice. The livestock must go with them. By this time Pharaoh was beside himself with anger. He shouted at Moses "Get out of my sight or I'll kill you!" "Don't worry," replied Moses, "I will go, and you will not see me again, ever!" *Exodus 5—10*

At the Pharaoh's continual refusal to allow the Hebrew slaves to go free, plague after disastrous plague came to the land. One plague was of frogs which left the polluted waters of the Nile in search of clean water. Many died in the hot sun and rotted. Locusts (below), grasshopper-like insects that destroy all vegetation in their path, were another of the plagues.

The Passover

THE TERRIBLE YEAR OF DISASTERS had left Egypt near to ruin. Her crops were wasted, her livestock sick and the people miserable and afraid. It was a high price to pay for resisting the God of Israel. But the year left Pharaoh more stubborn and more determined than ever to keep the slaves. It had become an obsession with him. He was king, he was a god, he would not obey his slaves' God.

The people were now ready, longing to leave Egypt for their own territory. The time had come for God to free his people; no Pharaoh had any power to stop them. So God told Moses about the last great disaster that was to befall the Egyptians and their Pharaoh.

Moses and Aaron then called the elders of the community together and outlined God's plan. They now knew that these men spoke God's words and were to be trusted and obeyed. Soon individual families were given their instructions and there was great excitement as the chosen day was whispered from family to family.

First, the people were to go to their Egyptian neighbours and ask to borrow gold, jewellery and clothes for their festival. Then, on the tenth of the month they were to prepare for the great escape. There would be no time for proper preparations for the desert journey, so each family was to select a healthy young sheep or kid to be slaughtered for their evening meal. But it was no normal dinner, as each mother and father explained to the children. The meat was to be roasted with bitter herbs to remind them how much they had suffered in Egypt. With the meal the families were to have bread made quickly, without any yeast. The rest of the dough should be put in their baking pans ready for the journey. Before the meal began each family had to be packed, ready to set off at a moment's notice.

By the evening of the fourteenth, the community at Goshen was buzzing with suppressed excitement as the families began their preparations. Each father took a knife and slit the throat of his lamb or kid, holding it over a bowl to catch the blood. Dipping a branch from a hyssop bush into the blood he solemnly brushed it over the beam above the door and down the doorposts. Then, the family went inside, shut their door and began to prepare the meal. The strange action was to save the lives of their sons.

Meanwhile, in the rest of Egypt the fateful night began quietly. No one suspected anything unusual. Pharaoh waited in his palace. He had been warned of God's terrible last sign but he would not believe it, neither would he change his mind.

Midnight came and suddenly a terrible wailing began in the Egyptian city. In family after family, death struck the eldest son! God had sent his angel of death into the land. No Egyptian family was spared. Even Pharaoh's son and heir died that night. The first-born male animals lay dead too. Only those in the houses with blood on their doorposts were safe. Not one Israelite son died, the angel passed over their houses, leaving them to eat the last meal in Egypt in safety.

Standing by the bedside of his dead son, Pharaoh knew that he could resist God no longer. He called Moses and Aaron to him in the middle of the night and stormed "Get out of my country. Take your families, your cattle, everything! But go *now*! But pray for me," he added in his misery. "I have sinned." The Egyptian people pleaded with the Israelites too. "Please go," they cried. "Leave the country before we all die."

The people of Israel were ready. Moses and Aaron gave the word at once and the whole tribe set out into the desert to return to the land God had promised them. There were nearly two million people as well as their sheep and goats. It had been 430 years since Jacob's family had settled in Egypt under Joseph's protection. Joseph's final request that he should go back to his homeland when God led the people out was fulfilled as his embalmed body was carried in a coffin in the place of honour.

The Israelites had a long way to go and many adventures and difficulties would come their way. But as they left Egypt their spirits were high. God had set them free. Whatever happened, they were no longer slaves. *Exodus 11–13*

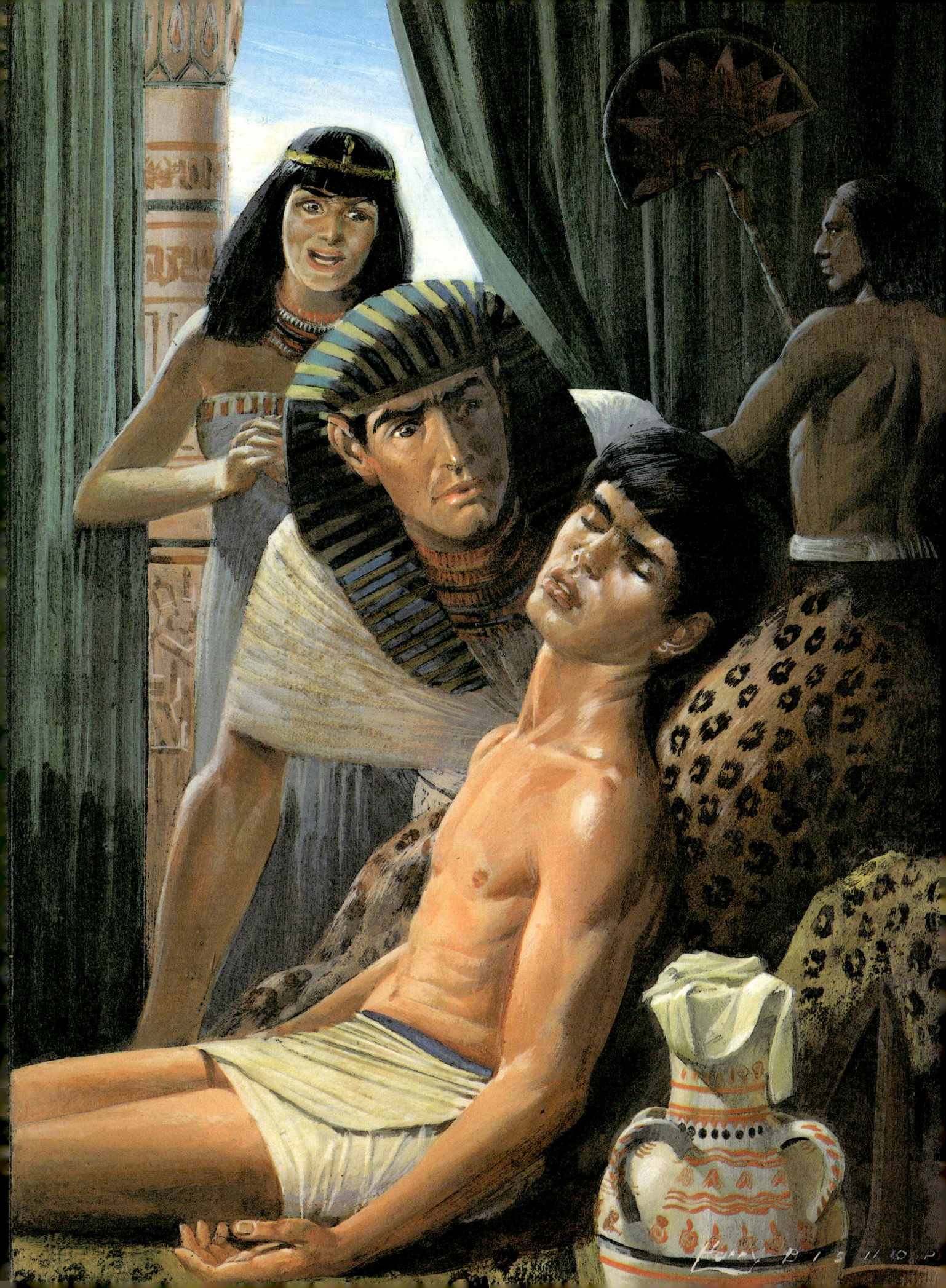

The Crossing of the Red Sea

WHEN THE ISRAELITES SET OFF into the desert, God gave them a sign to show that he was leading them on their historic journey. In the day they could clearly see a great column of cloud, like a pillar, at the head of the march. At night this became a bright column of fire.

The Israelites followed the column to the Red Sea or Sea of Reeds, part of the Bitter Lakes near their old home. But the escape was not as easy as they had hoped. As soon as they had left, Pharaoh regretted his decision. He and his people had lost their slaves. He decided to force them to return. The cruel ruler mobilized his armies and set off at the head of his crack unit of charioteers.

Meanwhile, Moses, at God's command, camped between a range of mountains and the edge of the Sea of Reeds. While they rested and ate, look-outs

paced the heights above. Suddenly they spotted the Egyptian forces in hot pursuit.

This was to be the Israelites' first test of faith in God. But instead of trust, they panicked and accused Moses and Aaron of throwing away their lives. Moses quietened them and said, "Don't be afraid. The Lord will fight for us."

Then God said to Moses, "Take your staff and raise it high over the sea." The Israelites crowded round as their leader stood on a rock and held his staff over the waters. As he did so, the pillar of cloud came between the Egyptians and the Israelites, creating a screen so that the army could not attack. All through the night Moses held his staff high and the Israelites noticed a steady east wind blowing across the water in front of them. By morning the water had drawn back to leave a roadway across the reed beds. At Moses' order the whole nation marched across the dry sea bed.

As morning came, the Egyptians broke through the cloud barrier. As the last Israelite family left the marshy area the Egyptians were in sight directly behind them. But God was firmly in control. The Egyptians' chariot wheels became stuck in the soft sea bed. While they were held up, God ordered Moses to raise his staff again. This time the water returned to its normal level with a mighty roar, catching the whole army in the middle of the sea and destroying it.

This miraculous escape restored the Israelites' faith in God and their confidence in Moses and Aaron. There were great celebrations in the camp that night. Moses led the people in a song of praise to God their deliverer. While the women danced, thousands of voices echoed round the coast. "Sing to the Lord because he has won a glorious victory," they roared. "He has thrown the horses and their riders into the sea." *Exodus 13–14*

The Long Journey

THE ISRAELITES WERE TIRED AND THIRSTY. They had been marching for three days since their escape from the Egyptians, and in all that time they had not found a drop of water in the desert. Their supplies were low and they were getting anxious. The next day, foraging parties found water at a place called Marah. People rushed to fill their water skins. But the water was bitter and undrinkable.

In their disappointment, the people turned on Moses. "What are we going to drink here in the desert?" they demanded. Again, Moses prayed to God. In answer, God guided Moses to a tree. Moses cut it down as he was told, took it to the bitter water and threw it in. Timidly people came to the pool's edge and tasted the water. It was crystal clear and drinkable!

So the great community set off again. The next stop was an oasis called Elim where there were twelve fresh springs and 70 palm trees. After they had rested, the people marched on into the desert of Sin, a harsh rocky wilderness.

The Hebrews soon forgot how God had cared for them and how faithfully Moses had led them so far. As food supplies dwindled and tempers frayed, they began accusing Moses of letting them down. "You've brought us out here to starve to death!" they shouted.

But God wasn't going to allow his people to starve. He told Moses: "I am going to make food drop from the sky so that they will be able to gather all they need. But I shall do it in such a way as to test whether they will follow my instructions."

Moses and Aaron called the community together and told them that God had heard their complaint. "Soon you will know that God is with us. You will see his light shining here in the desert and he has promised meat for you this very evening and as much bread as you need tomorrow morning". As the people gathered round, a dazzling light appeared in the clouds. The people knew that this was the powerful presence of God.

As evening approached, people became more excited, wondering how God was going to provide food for them. Suddenly a dark smudge appeared on the horizon. As it drew nearer, everyone could see that it was a great flock of birds. They were migrating quails and they had already flown thousands of miles. Tired from their journey, they landed close to the camp. The Israelites swooped on the exhausted birds. That night the smell of roasting quail filled the camp. God had kept the first part of his promise.

Early next morning, the people rushed out of their tents to see what God was going to give them for breakfast. There was nothing but a heavy dew on the ground round the camp. But as the sun grew hotter, the dew evaporated and left a white, flaky

substance like frost on the ground. The Israelites were puzzled. "What is it?" they asked. "This is manna", Moses told them. "It is the food God has sent you. Gather what you need. You can boil it, or bake it into bread, but remember you must use it up today. Leave none for tomorrow."

Soon everyone was out with their bowls and pots gathering the manna. It looked like small white seeds. It tasted delicious, like biscuits made with honey. The marvellous thing was that no matter how much or little people collected, it was just the right amount for the family. But there were some who thought they knew better than Moses and decided to keep some for the next day, in case God forgot them. Next morning they found that the manna had gone bad. In this way God used his gift to test whether people would obey him.

For five days the Hebrews collected the manna in the morning. Any that was left on the ground melted away as the sun grew hotter. On the sixth day Moses gave them more instructions. "Tomorrow is to be a special day of rest," he told them. "Every seventh day from now on will be a holy day, dedicated to God. No work will be done at all, but so that you can eat on the holy day, God has said that we can collect enough manna for two days. Eat what you need today and leave the rest for tomorrow. This time it will not go bad overnight."

The people collected two days' supply and there was no manna to be seen next day. From then on the manna came down for six days and was collected. On the seventh day the people did no work but worshipped God.

God told Moses to keep a jar of manna in a special place to show their descendants. This reminder of God's goodness was taken wherever the Israelites went.

Exodus 15–16

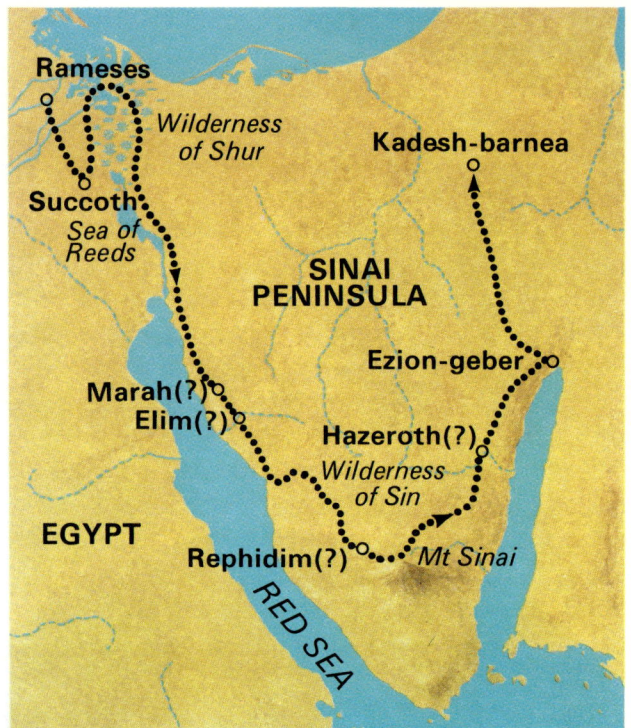

The probable route of the Exodus

Water from the Rock

THE ISRAELITES HAD PLENTY TO EAT as they journeyed on. But water became scarce as the desert landscape changed to the rocky foothills of the Sinai mountain range. One evening, as they pitched camp at a place called Rephidim, the Israelites began to complain again. There was no water for miles.

"Have you brought us all this way just to let us die?" they demanded of Moses. "Why must you keep complaining?" he asked. "Are you trying to test God?" But the people were so angry that Moses began to fear for his life. He went away and prayed to God for help.

Once more God told Moses how he could find water. He was to gather the leaders and take them into the mountains. There he would find a particular rock which he was to strike with his staff. He found the rock and as he struck it a spring of water gushed out and ran down the slope! The men were amazed. There was now enough water for everyone. God had shown yet again that he could be trusted.

One day, during their stay at Rephidim there was a shout from the lookouts. A hostile tribe, the Amalekites, were about to attack the camp.

Moses made hasty battle plans. He ordered Joshua, his chief of defence, to fight the Amalekites at dawn the next day. 'Meanwhile," he told Joshua, "I will go to the top of the mountain to pray." The camp was a bustle of activity as Joshua organized his men. He formed them into ranks and told them the plan of action.

By dawn the Hebrews were in position and Moses stood on a rocky peak overlooking the field of battle. Joshua's forces attacked and the Amalekites fought back. They were a tough, warlike people and the battle was fierce. But things went well for the Israelites. High above them they could see Moses, arms aloft and staff in hand, praying to God for victory.

So long as Moses held his arms aloft Joshua's forces gradually gained the upper hand. By sundown the Israelites had beaten the Amalekite army.

The victory boosted the spirits of the Israelite community. That night there was singing and dancing as the battered but cheerful heroes returned to the camp. They gave praise to God for saving them from their enemies.

The Israelites stayed at Rephidim for some time, and while they were there, Moses was reunited with his wife, Zipporah. She had travelled with his sons and his father-in-law, Jethro, all the way from Midian, having heard of the remarkable escape from Egypt. It was a happy reunion for the family.

Moses greatly respected his father-in-law and lost no time in telling him everything that had happened since the time he had left Midian to return to Egypt. Although he was not an Israelite, Jethro believed in Moses' God and was full of praises to God for the way he had rescued and looked after his son-in-law's people.

Moses as their leader, was also the Israelites' final authority on matters of law. Anyone with any kind of dispute, however small, brought it before him for judgment. Moses sat as judge and jury from dawn to dusk. It was exhausting work, and time was often wasted trying to sort out petty squabbles.

When Jethro saw this, he was astounded. "Why do you wear yourself out like this?" he asked. "I have to," Moses replied, simply. "The people need to know how God wants them to act in their daily lives, so they come to me. I tell them what God's laws and commands are."

Jethro was the leader of the Midianite tribe and he now gave Moses some advice. He said, "I'm sure that it is right to represent your people before God and teach them his laws, but you can't do it all. Appoint God-fearing, trustworthy men, who will not be bribed, to act as judges over the minor disputes. If they have a serious or difficult case, then they can refer it to you. In that way everyone's arguments will be settled, and you won't be burdened with all the detail."

Jethro's advice made sense and Moses was sure it had God's approval. He picked out people he could trust and established a system of permanent judges, each one over ten, fifty, a hundred or a thousand people.

Jethro stayed with the Israelites until Moses had set up his new legal system and then returned to his home in Midian.

Moses then ordered the people to pack everything together for the next stage of the journey. They were headed for Mount Sinai, the Holy Mountain, which marked the end of the first stage of their journey.

Two months after they had set off from Egypt, the great sprawling procession arrived in the mountains. They were to stay there for a whole year, during which time there were to be some dramatic events that would affect the whole future of the Israelite nation. *Exodus 17–18*

Moses on Mount Sinai

THE ISRAELITES SET UP CAMP at the foot of Mount Sinai and Moses climbed to the mountain's peak. On the mountain, God was going to establish a binding agreement with the people of Israel that would make them a special nation. He said to Moses, "I will make a solemn agreement with you all. The whole of the earth is mine, but you will be my chosen people. Your nation must keep my commandments and dedicate themselves to me only."

Moses returned to the people waiting below. He called the leaders together and explained what God had promised. They vowed, on behalf of the people, to keep their part of the agreement. "We will do everything God has said," they told Moses.

The old man returned to the mountain-top and told God of their promises, while the Israelites waited expectantly below. So God told Moses how to prepare for the dramatic moment when he would reveal his mighty presence to them. The Israelites were to wash their clothes as a sign of making themselves clean and pure before God. They were to make a boundary around the base of the holy mountain which the Israelites should not cross. If they did so they would die. Then they were to wait for a special sign to show that God was with them.

By the third day, everyone was ready and dressed in clean clothes. They waited with a mixture of excitement, curiosity and fear.

The Stone Tablets

The ten commandments, the summing up of God's laws for his people, were written on two flat stone 'tables' or tablets. They were called the 'tables of the covenant', and were kept in the most holy part of the Tabernacle, in the Ark of the Covenant. (Covenant means agreement.)

We do not know exactly how Moses received the tablets. The Bible states that they were 'written with the finger of God' and given to Moses on the mountain. This may be a literal description of what happened, or picture language to emphasize the fact that the commands came directly from God.

THE TEN COMMANDMENTS

And God spoke all these words, saying,
*   "I am the Lord your God, who brought*
you out of the land of Egypt, out of the
house of bondage.
*   "You shall have no other gods before me.*
*   "You shall not make for yourself a*
graven image, or any likeness of anything
that is in heaven above, or that is in
the earth beneath, or that is in the
water under the earth; you shall not bow
down to them or serve them.
*   "You shall not take the name of the*
Lord your God in vain.
*   "Remember the sabbath day, to keep it*
holy.
*   "Honour your father and your mother.*
*   "You shall not kill.*
*   "You shall not commit adultery.*
*   "You shall not steal.*
*   "You shall not bear false witness*
against your neighbour.
*   "You shall not covet your neighbour's*
house; you shall not covet your neighbour's
wife, or his manservant, or his
maidservant, or his ox, or his ass, or
anything that is your neighbour's.
Exodus 20

Suddenly a crash of thunder rolled out, louder than anything they had ever heard. Lightning flashed and a vast, dark cloud descended on the mountain top. A majestic trumpet blared and echoed around the mountainside. Everyone in the camp shook with fear, from the youngest child to the toughest soldier.

Then Moses led the people out of the camp to the foot of the mountain, just below the marked boundary. By now the whole mountain was covered with clouds of smoke, showing that God's presence was there.

The great trumpet fanfare grew even louder and Moses cried out to God. The Lord answered him in a voice of thunder. Then Moses went up to the mountain into the presence of Jehovah. He took Aaron with him but the people dared not approach the mountain. "You tell us what God says," they pleaded "If God speaks to us we will die."

High on the mountain, the Lord gave his commands to Moses. These commands became the laws by which the Israelites had to live if they were to remain God's chosen people. His laws did not just cover worship, but also the way people had to treat one another. Every part of their life fell under God's rules. They were contained in ten guidelines on how to behave. These have become the basis of law for many societies ever since.

The commandments were simple, yet profound. The Israelites were to worship no god other than God himself. They should not make idols or statues to worship, or misuse the name of God. Every seventh day should be kept as a rest day, dedicated to God and his worship.

Children were to respect and obey their parents. Murder was wrong, and so was adultery and stealing. Lies were not to be told against others and no one should be jealous of anyone because of what they owned.

If the people lived by these rules, treating their fellows with love and fairness, and continued to worship the Lord who made them, they would prosper.

God also gave Moses more detailed instructions on how people should live from day to day. Worship must be simple; altars were to be made from earth or uncut stone, not grand affairs of silver or gold.

The Israelites could be quick-tempered and violent in their quarrels, so punishments for violence and murder were to be strict. Murder and a number of other serious crimes carried the death penalty. For assault that caused injury, compensation had to be given.

There were laws dealing with injury, theft and damage to property, and also those to protect young girls from rape or seduction. Foreigners were not to be ill-treated and the poor were not to be made to pay high interest rates by money-lenders.

God told the Israelites to set aside part of their corn, wine and olive oil as an offering and that each first-born son should be dedicated to him. First-born cattle and sheep should be offered as a sacrifice to God.

God was determined that the people should live alongside one another in peace. He condemned the spreading of false rumours about innocent people, and all forms of bribery. His people must be responsible in their actions and always ready to help others.

God told Moses the annual religious festivals he wanted his nation to keep. They were the Feast of the Passover, which celebrated the nation's deliverance from Egypt by God, the Festival of Harvest and the Festival of Firstfruits, to be held in the autumn when the grapes were picked and collected for storage.

If his people were faithful, there would be blessings too. God would fight for them in battle, they would not be short of food or water, neither would they be stricken with diseases. The women of the community would have no difficulty in bearing children and people would live to a good old age.

When Moses came down the mountain, the Israelites fell silent as he gave them these instructions. Having seen the power of God the people answered immediately: "We will do everything God has said!" Moses then wrote down the commandments as a permanent record.

The next morning Moses built a special altar. On it he set twelve rocks, one for each of the tribes of Israel. Animals were killed for sacrifice on the altar. Moses took their blood and sprinkled half of it on the sides of the altar to signify God's part of the agreement. He splashed the other half over the people as a sign to show that they had made their promise too.

The ceremony over, Moses took Aaron, two of Aaron's sons and 70 of the Israelite leaders up the Holy Mountain with him. There they were given a privilege only a very few people in history have ever had. They were granted a vision of God. It seemed that beneath him stretched a dazzling pavement of sapphires, blue as a summer sky.

Then Aaron and the leaders rejoined the Israelites, full of everything they had seen and heard. But Moses returned to the peak where he was to stay in God's presence for 40 days and nights. As he climbed, a dense cloud covered the mountain again. From below it looked as if a fire was raging on the peak.

God gave Moses many more laws. The laws were engraved on stone tablets. "These tablets contain all the laws that I have given for the instruction of the people," God told Moses.

But at the very moment when Moses was sealing the agreement with God, the Israelites had begun to break it! *Exodus 19–24*

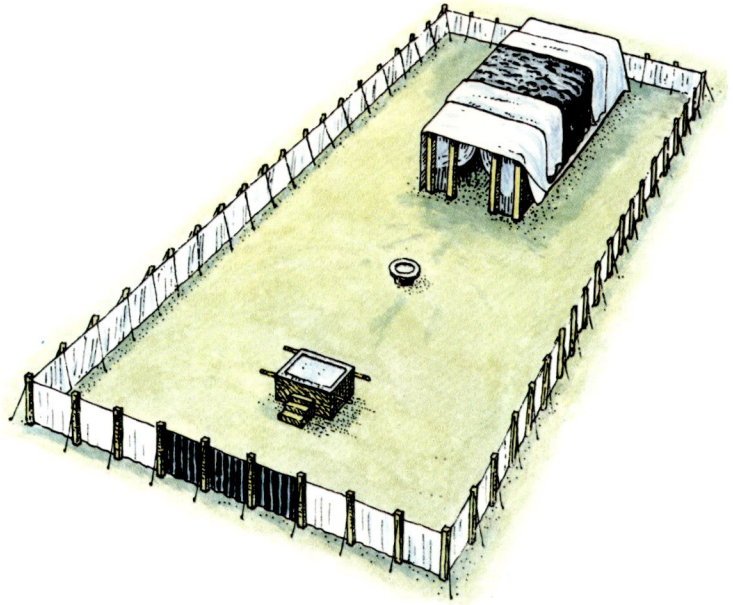

A reconstruction of what the Tabernacle or Tent of Meeting may have looked like. It was a portable shrine or chapel to which the Hebrew desert wanderers went to worship and seek God's direction. In it was kept the Ark of the Covenant.

High priests wore special robes with a breastplate studded with twelve jewels, one for each of the twelve tribes.

The Golden Calf

MOSES HAD BEEN ON THE MOUNTAIN for nearly six weeks and the Israelites were getting impatient. They decided that Moses had deserted them. Because Moses was their only link with God, they thought that the Lord had gone too, leaving them alone and leaderless to face the desert and the mountains.

A group of them started putting pressure on Aaron. "Moses has gone, but we don't know where," they said. "We must have a god to lead us." Aaron was losing control of the situation and panicked. He was not strong enough to take the lead himself and a people without a god in those days was thought to be easy prey for the warlike tribes of the desert.

Aaron gave into their demands and said: "Bring me the gold earrings belonging to your wives and children." He collected all the metal together, made a mould and cast a magnificent golden bull calf. When the people saw it they were overjoyed. "At last, a god we can see. This is our god," they shouted. "It was he who led us out of Egypt." Aaron should have known better but he was caught up in the excitement and made an altar so that sacrifices could be made to the golden calf. The next day there was feasting around the image and an orgy of pagan worship.

Meanwhile, up on the mountain peak, God knew what was going on. He was angry that the Israelites should so easily break the promises they had made only six weeks before. God showed Moses how his tribe was behaving. Totally ashamed for them, Moses could only plead for their lives before God. With a heavy heart, Moses returned to the Israelites carrying the two tablets of stone on which the law of God was written.

When he arrived at the foot of the mountain he was horrified to see the orgy still raging. Here were his people, who knew so much about the living God, bowing down to a metal image. Moses raised his hands and smashed the stone tablets down on the ground. They shattered with a mighty crash. The agreement had been broken.

As Moses stormed into the camp all the festivities stopped. The people suddenly realized what they had done. Moses took the golden idol and ordered it to be melted down. Taking the gold, he had it pounded to dust. It was mixed with water and the people were made to drink it!

Nervously, Aaron came up to Moses. He tried to excuse his actions but his story was weak. He claimed that he had thrown the earrings into the fire and the bull had appeared like magic! Moses was stony-faced. The people had to be punished. They had broken the law. He stood at the gate of the camp and shouted, "Everyone who is on the Lord's side, come to me!" The tribe of Levi, as one man, came to his side. They alone had refused to worship the bull god. Moses ordered this faithful few to kill the offenders.

With heavy hearts the Levites strode into the camp and put to the sword 3,000 of their own people that day. Because they had remained faithful to God's cause, Moses made the Levites the Lord's priests, a family privilege that was to be theirs for centuries.

Now Moses was in charge again, the people were happy to follow the laws of God and the guidance of their leader. For the last time, on the peak of Mount Sinai, God gave Moses a glimpse of his majestic and terrifying greatness. Moses took with him two more stone tablets to replace the broken ones. Again God's law was engraved on them to show that the agreement between God and the people was renewed.

When Moses returned to the camp after this meeting, his face reflected the glory of God. It shone with a radiance only possible in someone who had been in the presence of God. It so frightened the people of Israel that he had to cover his face with a veil. Then Moses gave his people instructions to break camp and head, once more, for the desert. *Exodus 32*

False gods

The Israelites believed in only one God, yet they often deserted him and turned to the worship of the 'false gods' of their neighbours. Their worship of the Golden Calf is just one instance of their disloyalty. The Old Testament is full of the raging anger of prophets condemning them for their lack of faith and warning them of the consequences of bowing down before idols.

Spies into Canaan

HOWEVER MUCH THE ISRAELITE NATION disobeyed God and broke their agreement with him, they were still his people. He continued to guide and care for them because he had chosen them.

God told Moses to construct a sacred tent which they could carry with them. Using the most beautiful and precious materials, together with the skills of the most talented designers and craftsmen among them, they were to make a tabernacle for their God.

When Moses told the people about it, they were enthusiastic. Each family gave some of the treasures they had brought from Egypt: gold, silver, bronze, fine linen, woven wool in blue, purple and red, the best leather, soft sheepskin and precious stones.

There were many skilled workmen in the tribe, but two were outstanding. Their names were Bezalel and Oholiab. These two men were chosen to be in charge of the whole project.

Bezalel and Oholiab gathered together a team of fine craftsmen and set to work. God had outlined the plans to Moses and working to these, the craftsmen built the most splendid tent imaginable. The walls were wooden planks, plated with gold,

The Ark of the Covenant was a wooden chest overlaid with gold. In it were kept the stone tablets of the law. At each corner were rings through which poles could be fitted so that the Ark could be carried about as the Hebrews travelled through the desert into Canaan. The winged figures on the lid, or mercy seat, are cherubim. They serve as a throne for Jehovah. The Ark was especially sacred for it was a sign of God's presence.

and the roof was cloth and animal skin. It could be taken down and carried with the Israelites as they travelled.

In the centre of this tent or tabernacle, in its own special inner room, they put the Ark or Covenant Box, made from acacia wood and gold. In it were kept the stone tablets of the law, a jar of manna and Aaron's special staff. This box became special to the Israelites and was carried with great care and ceremony wherever they went. It was a sign that God was always with them.

When the tent was finished, and had been dedicated to God, the same cloud and dazzling light came down over it as had appeared over Mount Sinai. God was with his people.

Aaron and his sons (part of the tribe of Levi) were now dedicated to special office as God's priests. Aaron, as High Priest, was given ceremonial robes to wear, with a breastplate studded with twelve jewels, one for each of the twelve tribes.

One morning, eleven months after they had first come to Sinai, the cloud lifted from above the sacred tent. The Israelites knew it was time to be moving on. They broke camp and began their journey once again. The Covenant Box and furled tent were carried in a place of honour at the head of the march.

The journey was not an easy one. It was marked by constant grumblings, troubles and even minor rebellions. Moses' patience was put to the test many times.

At last they came to the borders of Canaan, in sight of their homeland. It seemed a daunting task to conquer and take possession of the territory. The people asked Moses to send spies to report on the land. To reassure them, Moses agreed. Twelve agents set out into Canaan on a spying mission.

Forty days later they returned. Two of the spies, Joshua and Caleb, were optimistic. They reported that it was rich farming land. They even brought back a bunch of grapes so large and heavy that they had to carry it between them. But the other spies were more concerned with the strength of the people living there. The local tribes were armed and fierce, they reported. There was even some talk of giants! But Moses remained confident that God would help them overcome any opposition. However, rumours began to spread among the people. "The land is dreadful! It doesn't produce enough for the people there already, let alone us. It is full of giants who could crush us like grasshoppers!" The Israelites came very close to rebellion.

As Moses and Aaron stood before them, pleading with the people to see sense, an angry cry went up. "Let's choose another leader," they shouted. "Someone who will take us back to the comforts of Egypt."

The Israelites had become an angry mob. People stooped down to pick up rocks. They were ready to stone their leaders to death.

Just in time, the shining light of God's presence came down on the tent and the people stopped. God was furious with the Israelites and might well have destroyed the disobedient there and then. Instead, he promised that none of those people involved in the rebellion would ever see the Promised Land.

So began 40 years of travel in the desert before God would allow the Israelites to enter their home.

Once more the Israelites moved off into the desert and pitched camp. There was no water to be found and so they turned to Moses again. God told Moses and Aaron to take the staff from the Covenant Box. He directed them to a water-bearing rock and instructed them to speak to the rock. This time it was Moses who disobeyed. Raising the staff above his head he struck the rock twice, as he had done before. Water gushed out, but God was angry with Moses and Aaron. Neither of them, he

said, would lead the people into the Promised Land.

Before long Aaron died and his position as High Priest was taken by his son Eleazar. Despite their complaints, Aaron was loved and respected by the people and they mourned his death.

The Israelites continued to be rebellious and to accuse God of failing to look after them. They even complained that they were bored with the manna he sent them every day. Then they were in trouble.

A vast plague of poisonous snakes hit the camp. Many of the Israelites were bitten and died. Others cried out to Moses. "We should never have doubted the Lord! Please, please, ask God to take these snakes away!"

Moses acted quickly. At God's command, he made a snake out of bronze and fixed it on a pole. Holding it up high, where everyone could see it, he shouted: "Look at the bronze snake and you will be saved."

Miraculously it happened. Those who, only minutes before, had been at death's door, fixed their eyes on the snake and were healed. The snakes left the camp. God had punished his people, but he had not destroyed them. There was always salvation for those who were prepared to trust his promises. *Exodus 35–40; Numbers 13, 20, 21*

Harry Bishop

Balaam's Ass

BALAAM WAS SITTING IN HIS HOUSE reading his scrolls. He was a prophet who lived far away to the east of Canaan in Mesopotamia. He had the power to put curses on people and was feared and respected by kings and tribal leaders. He was usually happy to provide curses or blessings to order, depending on how much he was paid. But he knew that the Israelite's God, Jehovah, was the all-powerful God of the whole world. If God spoke, he must do as he said.

One day important messengers came to see Balaam. They were men from the tribes of Moab and Midian, sent by King Balak the Midianite leader who was worried about the Israelites. The messengers delivered this message from Balak: "The Israelites are threatening to take over the lands. I want you to put a curse on them so that we can drive them away." The messengers had plenty of money to pay for Balaam's services.

That night Balaam had a dream in which God told him that Israel was his own chosen nation. Under no circumstances was he to curse them. So next morning Balaam sent the messengers away with a refusal.

But King Balak was not to be put off easily. He sent more important envoys with even more money. Balaam told them that all the money in the world would be no use to him if he disobeyed God.

That night God spoke to him again. He said: "You may go, but you must only say what *I* tell you to." So next morning Balaam saddled his donkey and set off with King Balak's men.

While he was riding along the road, his donkey suddenly lurched off the road into a field. Balaam, angry at his normally placid donkey, beat the animal with his stick. He could not see what the donkey could see. The Angel of the Lord stood barring the road ahead.

As the angel moved, the donkey moved forward again. Then the angel stopped and the donkey pressed into the side of the road to get out of the way, crushing Balaam's foot against the stone wall.

The prophet who still could not see the angel was furious with the animal and beat him again.

The angel moved to an even narrower stretch of the road, blocking it completely. Frightened and bewildered, the donkey just gave up and lay down in the road. Balaam set about the poor beast with his stick. Then he heard the donkey speak: "What have I done to deserve this treatment?" Surprised, Balaam shouted back, "You've made a fool out of me, that's what!" Suddenly, Balaam could see the angel! At once he realized that this divine messenger was sent to remind him that God was watching him.

When Balaam and his party arrived, King Balak took him to a hill where he could see the Israelites. All was ready for Balaam to put his curse on the Israelite nation. But Balaam was aware of the God of Israel protecting his people. He knew they must be blessed, not cursed. So summoning up his courage, Balaam made a great ceremonial speech in praise of Israel and their God.

Balak was confused. Was he paying this man good money so that he could bless his enemy and give them an advantage? He took Balaam to another place to try again, but Balaam told the king: "I can only do what God tells me to", and he recited another wonderful poem, blessing the Israelites. Balak was losing his patience. He tried a third time, but with no success.

By now Balak was at the end of his tether. This man persisted in doing exactly the opposite of what he was asked. In despair, he ordered Balaam to leave. But Balaam, speaking with the authority God gave him, began to predict the future. He told everyone that one day a great and mighty king would come to rule over Israel, someone who would lead them to victory!

Balak saw all his hopes of victory dashed. He sent Balaam home without any payment and returned to his tribe. He knew that there was no sense in fighting the people God had chosen.

Numbers 22—23

41

The Death of Moses

OSES WAS GROWING OLD. Although still fit and strong, he knew he did not have long to live. The Israelite nation was at last poised to cross the river Jordan from the plains of Moab and to enter the land they had been promised so many years before. Moses knew he would not enter the land himself, because of his failure to obey God's command when he struck the rock.

On the eve of their entry into Canaan, Moses was instructed to take a census of all the fit and able men over the age of 20 who were eligible for military service. (The tribe of Levi, the priests, were exempt from fighting.) The Israelite army numbered almost 602,000 men, but there was not one man left alive of those who had mistrusted God when spies were first sent into the land. Only Joshua and Caleb, the two spies to remain faithful to God, had survived the 40 years in the desert.

Because he was going to die, Moses asked God to appoint a man to lead the people. God chose Joshua, Moses' right-hand man. He was a capable commander, who loved and trusted God.

So Moses gathered the people together and said: "I am 120 years old and no longer able to be your leader. I will not go with you to the Promised Land, but God will be with you. You will overcome the nations that live there and make the land your own. You need not fear the tribes. Be confident! God our father will not abandon you!"

Then Moses turned to Joshua, who knelt before Moses. He placed his hands on Joshua's head and declared to the whole nation that he was to be their new leader. Next he called Eleazar, the High Priest who would interpret God's commands for the nation. He would be with Joshua to lead the people. The tribe shouted their approval.

When the ceremony was over, Moses and Joshua went to the sacred tent where the dazzling light and cloud of God's presence hovered. There they heard God's special instructions. Leading the Israelites would not be easy. They would rebel once more when they entered the land and would turn their backs on God yet again. Joshua would need all God's wisdom and strength for the task.

The Lord gave Moses and Joshua a hymn or national anthem for the people. It spoke of how God had chosen the Israelite nation for himself and protected and cared for them in the desert, "like an eagle, teaching its young to fly."

Finally, Moses set out for Mount Pisgah to meet God for the last time on earth. Before he went, he spoke for the last time to his people: "God's commands are not empty words," he told them, "they are your very life, the pattern you should live by, always." Then, with a special word of blessing and encouragement for each of the twelve tribes of Israel, and promising great things for the nation, he left them.

At the peak of the mountain, God showed Moses the land he would never reach, stretching out into the distance.

Soon after this last meeting with God, Moses died. The Israelites never saw him again and to this day, no one has ever discovered Moses' grave.

So ended one dramatic period of Israel's history. Despite slavery, ruthless enemies, hardship, disease and rebellion, the nation had survived. It was on the threshold of a new era under a new leader. As the great tribe, with their flocks of sheep, goats and cattle stood ready to cross the river Jordan, their spirits were high. The Promised Land lay ahead.

Deuteronomy 34

Harry BISHOP

GLOSSARY

ALTAR a place for offering sacrifices to God. Israelite altars were usually simple mounds of earth or uncut stone.

BALM sweet-smelling ointment used to soothe and heal.

BRIBE persuade someone to act illegally by offering him money.

CARAVAN an armed group of traders and travellers on camels and pack donkeys. Usual method of travel in the desert.

COMMISSION give someone a special job to do.

COMPENSATION payment made for loss or damage to property.

EMBALM method of preserving bodies for burial.

EPIDEMIC disease spreading rapidly to large numbers of people.

FESTIVAL celebration of an important event in the past.

FOREMAN worker in charge of, and representing, his fellow-workers.

HIGH PRIEST leader of the Temple priests. Allowed to enter the Holy of Holies to offer the annual sacrifices on the Day of Atonement.

HYMN a religious song, usually used in worship.

HYSSOP a bush, similar to the herb, marjoram. It was used like a brush by the Hebrews in cleansing ceremonies and at Passover.

IDOL image of a god in wood, stone or metal. Used as a focus for worship.

IMMIGRANT settler in a foreign country.

LEASE paying to borrow land or goods for a fixed period of time.

MANNA may have been a sweet substance produced by the tamarisk tree. The word manna, means "what is it?"

MIDWIFE woman skilled in helping with the birth of babies.

MOURNING period of remembrance and sorrow at someone's death. For the Israelites it was one week. Egyptians mourned an important person for 72 days.

NIGHTMARE a strange or frightening dream. Egyptians believed they were to warn the dreamer about the future.

NOMADS people who travel with their livestock from pasture to pasture, never staying for long in one place.

OASIS a place where water naturally occurs in the desert. Sometimes inhabited, used as a stopping-place for travellers.

OFFERING money, food or animals given to God.

PHARAOH title given to kings of Egypt.

PITCH waterproof coating of tar.

PROPHET inspired teacher or interpreter of God's will; often able to predict the future.

QUAIL a small bird found throughout the Middle East. Twice a year, large numbers migrate across the desert.

SACRIFICE something offered to God as an expression of thanks. Sometimes a freshly killed animal is offered on an altar as a sign of repentance.

SILO a large dry bottle-shaped pit dug in the ground, used as a storage place for grain. Larger city silos may have been above ground and chimney-shaped.

TABLET stone, cut with a flat surface, on which lettering can be carved.

THE NAMES OF GOD

As people began to learn more about God, they developed a number of different ways of speaking about him. In Bible times, names were very important.

The earliest general name for a god was EL. This name was used for any god or image, good or evil, worshipped by a tribe or people.

In those earliest times, God was called ELYON or EL ELYON, the most High God. People believed that there were many gods in the world, but ELYON was above them all. By Abraham's time, God was called ELOHIM, the one supreme God.

As well as these words for God, the people had a name for him, YAHWEH or Jehovah. This name was so holy that nobody spoke it. Instead, they used the word ADONAI, or Lord.

YAHWEH comes from the Hebrew word for "to be" and means that God is with his people for all time and even beyond time. He is eternal. So, to Moses, at the burning bush God described himself, as I AM.

FOUNDERS OF THE JEWISH FAITH

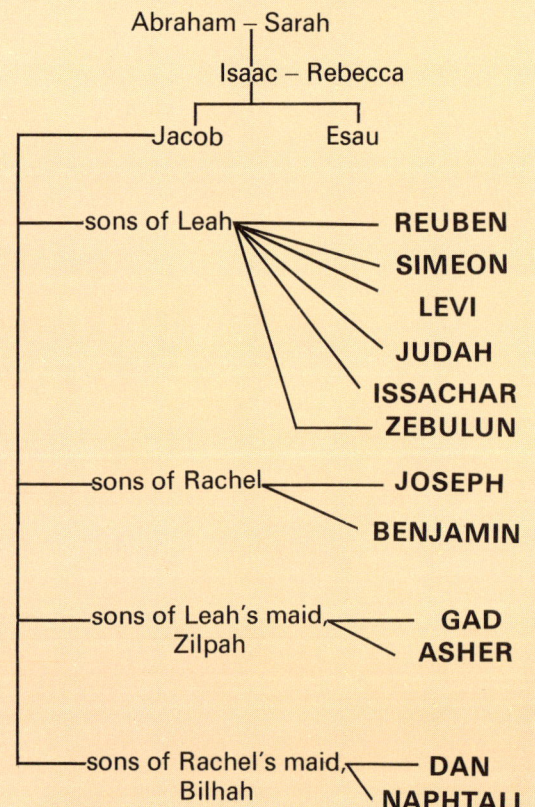

Abraham – Sarah

Isaac – Rebecca

Jacob   Esau

sons of Leah
- REUBEN
- SIMEON
- LEVI
- JUDAH
- ISSACHAR
- ZEBULUN

sons of Rachel
- JOSEPH
- BENJAMIN

sons of Leah's maid, Zilpah
- GAD
- ASHER

sons of Rachel's maid, Bilhah
- DAN
- NAPHTALI

The sons of Jacob founded the 12 tribes of Israel.

DATE CHART INDEX

The stories behind the events shown on the chart are told in the first five books of the Old Testament: Genesis, Exodus, Leviticus, Numbers and Deuteronomy. The dates are approximate.

BC	EGYPT	ISRAEL
1800	End of middle kingdom 1786	Jacob lives.
1750	Hyksos kings rule 1710–1570	Jacob's son, Joseph banished to Egypt.
1650	**New kingdom begins 1570–1085**	Jacob's family settle in Egypt.
1500	Tuthmosis III 1490–1437	
1400	Amenophis III 1390–1353	
	Amenophis IV/ Akhenaten 1361–1345	
1360		Birth of Moses.
	XIXth Dynasty	
	Rameses I 1303–1302	
	Sethos I 1302–1290	
1280	Rameses II 1290–1224	**Exodus from Egypt begins.** Forty years in the Wilderness.
1240		Moses receives the 10 commandments. Moses dies.
		Israel crosses the Jordan into Canaan.

BLACK SEA

• Hattusa

HITTITE
KINGDOM

Halys

*Lake
Tuz*

TAURUS MOUNTAINS

Carchemish •

• Haran

Orontes

Euphrates

CYPRUS

THE GREAT SEA
(MEDITERRANIAN SEA)

Byblos •

Sidon •

PHOENICIA

• Damascus

Tyre •

• Dan

Megiddo •

Dothan •

Jordan

• Penuel

Shechem •

Bethel •

• Ai

Jerusalem •

• Jericho

Bethlehem •

CANAAN

*Dead
Sea*

Gaza •

• Hebron

4

Beer-sheba •

MOAB

EGYPT

5

2

Kadesh-
barnea

EDOM

• On

• Memphis

**Pyramids near
Memphis**

SINAI
PENINSULA

• Ezion-geber

**Moses receiving the
tablets of law on
Mount Sinai**

3

Nile

1. Joseph interprets
   Pharaoh's dreams
   and is made a
   powerful official in
   Egypt.

2. The Hebrews, led by
   Moses, escape from
   Egypt across the Sea
   of Reeds.

3. The Hebrews, led by
   Moses, wander in the
   desert for 40 years.

4. After many years
   Moses leads his
   people to Canaan,
   the Promised Land,
   but dies just in sight
   of it.

5. The Hebrews dwelt
   in bondage in the
   land of Goshen.

"The Promised Land"
Moses led the Hebrews to Canaan, "The Promised
Land" some time during the 13th century BC. The
pharaoh who ruled Egypt at the time of the Exodus
was probably Rameses II.

RED SEA